GREAT BASIN

BY
Phyllis Root and
Maxine McCormick

We wish to thank Marcia Phillips, Park Ranger at Great Basin National Park, and Glenn Atwood, a former Ranger at the park, for all their help. Also, thanks to George Shaw, Associate Professor of Geophysics at the University of Minnesota. Any errors are our own.

PUBLISHED BY
CRESTWOOD HOUSE
Mankato, MN, U.S.A.

LIBRARY OF CONGRESS CATALOGING IN PUBLICATION DATA

Root, Phyllis.
   Great Basin

(National parks)
Includes index.
   SUMMARY: Describes the geography and plant and animal life of Nevada's Great Basin National Park. Includes a history of the park and a map.
   1. Great Basin National Park (Nev.) — Juvenile literature. [1. Great Basin National Park (Nev.) 2. National parks and reserves.] I. McCormick, Maxine. II. Title. III. Series: National parks (Mankato, Minn.)
F847.G73R66   1988   979.3—dc19   88-18645
ISBN 0-89686-410-3

International Standard Book Number:	Library of Congress Catalog Card Number:
0-89686-410-3	88-18645

PHOTO CREDITS

Cover: DRK Photo: Tom Bean
DRK Photo: (Tom Bean) 4, 7, 9, 10-11, 12, 15, 16-17, 18, 19, 21, 22, 24, 26-27, 28, 31, 33, 34-35, 36, 38-39, 42

The recipe for pine-nut cookies is from *The Piñon Pine* by Ronald Lanner (Reno: University of Nevada Press, 1981.) Copyright © 1981 by Ronald Lanner. Used by permission of the publisher.

Produced by Carnival Enterprises.

CRESTWOOD HOUSE

Box 3427, Mankato, MN, U.S.A. 56002

TABLE OF CONTENTS

Great Basin National Park

MOUNTAINS IN THE DESERT

High in the mountains of Great Basin National Park, bristlecone pine trees cling to the rocks. Some of these trees are more than 3,000 years old. Bristlecone pines are the oldest living things on earth.

The park is on the Snake Mountain Range on the eastern edge of Nevada. The Snake Mountains are part of the basin and range country. This is a land of long, skinny mountain ranges. Miles and miles of desert lie between them. The mountains spring up like islands in a desert sea.

In this dry land the mountains burst with life. The mountains have risen high enough to snag the clouds that carry precious rain. The Snake Mountain Range is cool and green. Bobcats prowl, mule deer roam, and golden eagles soar. From desert to mountaintop, the park holds several different zones of life.

Wheeler Peak, the highest peak in the park, rises 13,063 feet. Streams weave their way down the mountain. Long ago, glaciers carved a huge hollow in its side.

The mountains hide many caves. Some are vast and dazzling, some narrow and muddy. Some are painted with pictures hundreds of years old.

A limestone arch high enough to ride a horse under rises in the park. The only glacier in the Great Basin sits high on Wheeler Peak.

Only a few types of wildflowers can grow on the top of Wheeler Peak.

In spring a wave of color moves up the mountains. Yellow asters, locoweed, and thistle-poppy bloom first on the lower slopes. As the snows melt, flowers bloom higher and higher on the mountains. In the fall the wave comes down the mountains. The leaves high on the mountains turn color first. Then the trees on the lower slopes blaze with autumn.

Great Basin National Park has trails to follow and mountains to climb. It has been called the loneliest park in America. The land is rugged, the mountains stunning. In the vast space, there is time to be alone with the silence and the beauty.

THE OLDEST LIVING THINGS ON EARTH

High on Wheeler Peak bristlecone pine trees grow. The land is rocky and the soil is thin. Little rain falls. Winter winds and snow blast the trees. The temperature is below freezing from November through April. Even in the summer the air is cool. Not many other trees can grow this high up.

Yet somehow the bristlecones survive. Their scientific name means "long-lived pines" (they are called bristlecones because sharp black "bristles" grow on the cones). Several groves of bristlecone pines are scattered through the park.

Bristlecone pines that grow at lower elevations grow straight and tall. Some may even reach 60 feet. Those that grow at *tree line* are short and twisted. They are only 15 feet high. Their trunks still keep growing thicker, however.

Sometimes the trees grow in clumps. The seeds of a clump were probably buried together by a bird. As the trees grew, their trunks touched and grew together. Now they look like one great tree.

Ancient bristlecone pines grow only in the harshest places. The air they grow in is very dry and cold. Little rain falls. The soil is poor. Not much else can grow.

These trees grow far apart from each other. They seem like islands. They do not have to fight other trees for water or sun. Bristlecone pines can take their time and grow very slowly. Scientists think this is why they live so long.

Bristlecone pine trees grow for thousands of years.

6

Bristlecone pine trees add one ring a year to their trunks. Scientists can tell how old a tree is by boring a long, slender core out of the side of the trunk. This boring does little harm to the tree. By studying the cores from living and dead trees, scientists can count how many years the tree has lived.

FROM SEED TO SPLENDID TREE

Bristlecones grow from seeds. These seeds are in dark purple cones. The dark color helps them soak up sun, so they can open sooner. In the fall, wind scatters the seeds. Sometimes birds bury the seeds for winter food. These buried seeds are most likely to sprout.

The trees grow slowly. Young bristlecones look strong and green. They are still called *saplings* when they are 50 years old. They are still young at 500 years old. Most of the bristlecones alive today are over 1,000 years old. A few bristlecone pines in Great Basin National Park are older than 3,000 years. In the White Mountains of California, the oldest known tree on earth grows. This bristlecone pine is 4,600 years old. Even the old trees grow new cones.

The trees have many ways of surviving in their cold, windy world. Their sap protects them from insects and disease. Their needles live for 20 to 40 years. The trees do not have to grow new needles every year. In bad years they do not produce any cones at all.

One reason bristlecones live so long is that most of their trunks and branches die in hard times. The oldest trees have only one thin strip of living bark and green needles growing on a massive, dead trunk. Some of their roots have died. As part of a tree dies, the bark falls off in strips. Sand and ice eat away at the wood. The tree looks bare and dead, but is still alive. It takes thousands of years for a bristlecone to die.

When it finally dies, a tree can remain standing for hundreds of years. Finally, water erodes soil from the roots of the tree, and it topples. Even when it falls, it does not rot. The air is too dry. Instead, wind, snow, ice, and sand wear away the tree. A bristlecone pine tree may lie on the ground for 4,000 years before it is worn away by wind-driven ice.

Ancient bristlecone pine trees grow in earth that is thin and rocky.

DEATH OF A TREE

Once the oldest living thing on earth grew on Wheeler Peak. This tree was 21 feet around at the ground but only 17 feet tall. It was almost 4,900 years old.

When this tree first sprouted, Egyptians were building the pyramids. People were learning how to make tools from metal instead of from stone and bone.

The tree was already 3,000 years old when Christ was born. It was over 4,000 years old when Columbus bumped into America.

Native Americans taught the Pilgrims how to plant corn. Still the tree grew. The colonies fought for their freedom. Still it grew. Lincoln freed the slaves. Two wars tore the world apart. Still the tree grew.

Some parts of the bristlecone pine tree may look dead—but the tree is still alive.

In 1964, a student doing research asked to cut down the tree. The Forest Service gave permission. The tree trunk had 4,844 growth rings. That tree was the oldest living thing on earth. People were outraged when they found

out the tree had been cut down.

Today the trees are protected in the park. Polished and gnarled, they will watch over the mountains for thousands of years.

THE DRY, COLD DESERT

The Great Basin lies in the rain shadow of the Sierra Nevada Mountains of eastern California. This means the mountains rise so high they steal the rain from the clouds that blow in from the Pacific Ocean. This makes most of Nevada a desert. Only about ten inches of rain and snow fall each year. Even in the desert, it snows.

The only places that get more rain and snow are the tall mountain ranges

Backpackers hiking on Wheeler Peak need sturdy shoes and warm clothes.

like the Snake Range. They are high enough to catch some moisture from the clouds. The mountains are full of animals and plants, rivers and lakes.

UP AND DOWN THE MOUNTAIN

In Great Basin National Park, desert rattlesnakes and golden eagles find homes. Desert sagebrush and alpine meadows grow. Walking up a mountain in the park is like passing through different worlds.

Higher on the mountain the *climate* changes. Climate is the kind of weather that happens in a place throughout the year. Different plants and animals need different climates to live. Deer can live in several climates. Sagebrush grouse can live in only one.

Animals like bighorn sheep never cross the desert. They spend their lives on the mountain. But birds come and go. Jays, crows, larks, woodpeckers, hawks, owls, and golden eagles stay the year round. Others such as mountain bluebirds, doves, and hummingbirds migrate. Over 140 kinds of birds have made their homes in the park. The mountains, forests, and meadows are sweet with their songs.

DESERT LIFE

In the desert climate, plants such as sagebrush and rabbitbrush grow. Fuzzy bee flies hover over the flowers. Sometimes after a rain the desert smells like sagebrush. There are no trees—the desert is too dry for them to grow.

Jackrabbits and pocket mice like the dry land. So do sagebrush grouse. These large birds live on the desert ground. Small herds of pronghorn roam among the brush and grassy plains.

The pronghorn is native to America. Its common name is "antelope." But the pronghorn is not related to the antelope of Asia or Africa. It is called pronghorn because a short prong juts out halfway up its horn.

The pronghorn's natural home is the desert. Here, speed and keen eyesight

FUN FACT The Snake Range may have gotten its name because of the Native Americans' love of baked snake.

help it escape from its enemies. It has large eyes and long lashes that help protect its eyes from the sun.

Pronghorns are the fastest hoofed animals in America. They can run steadily at 20 to 30 miles an hour. A pronghorn can even reach a speed of 70 miles an hour for a short distance.

Sagebrush is their main food. But they also come onto the grassy mountains in the park to graze. Fawns are born in May and June. One-week-old fawns can outrun a human.

At one time there were 35 million pronghorns. By 1924, they were almost extinct. Today, they are making a comeback.

Pronghorns share the desert with many other animals, including snakes, coyotes, badgers, and the big-eared, sharp-faced kit fox.

THE PYGMY FOREST

Above the desert the trees begin. The lower slopes of the mountains in Great Basin National Park are dry. Single-leaf piñon (pronounced pin-yan) and juniper trees grow far apart to soak up the meager rain. Most trees are less than 30 feet high. This area is called a *pygmy forest* because the trees are so short. Mule deer, striped skunks, mice, and ground squirrels find a home in this forest.

A Native American story explains why the trees are short. Long ago, the people were hungry. Wolf-god scattered pine nuts and made a forest grow. But the people were so weak from hunger they could not climb the trees. So Wolf-god tore the tops off the piñon pines and dwarfed the trees. Then the people could reach the pine nuts and eat them.

Piñon pine cones have large nuts inside. These are a rich food for mice, squirrels, chipmunks, birds, and people.

The early people who lived in the Great Basin area got much of their winter food from the piñon pine. A grove of piñon trees might have one good crop every three to seven years. So the people traveled to a different grove on a different mountain each fall.

Many small groups of people gathered together for the pine nut harvest. There they would knock the cones off the trees with hooked sticks and gather them into baskets. Heat from the sun or a fire dried the cones so they would

Many animals—and people—eat the nuts found in the piñon pine cone.

open. The nuts inside the cones were stored for the winter.

One animal that eats pine nuts also plants new pine trees. The piñon jay, a slate-blue bird, pecks the cones loose from the tree and hammers them apart. Then the jay stores the seeds in its throat and carries them to its nesting area, which may be as far as six miles away. There the jay buries the seeds in the ground for eating in winter. Some of these buried seeds sprout and grow into new piñon trees.

THE TALL FOREST

Above the pygmy forest pine needles carpet the ground. Pine trees, fir trees, aspen trees, and mountain mahogany grow up the mountain slopes.

FUN FACT   The piñon jay can hold about 25 seeds in his gullet at one time and can fly this load up to five miles before burying it in the soil.

Because the land is dry, piñon and juniper trees grow apart from each other.

16

Mountain mahogany looks like a tree, but it is really a bush. It is part of the rose family. One mahogany bush on Wheeler Peak is 28 feet tall and 13 feet around. It may be the largest mountain mahogany in the world. In other parts of Nevada these bushes were burned for mining. But on Wheeler Peak they have never been cut.

In places the aspen trees grow in groves. Their leaves, green on top and silver below, shimmer in a breeze. In the summer, mule deer and their fawns live in the aspen groves and evergreen forest. In autumn, they leave the forest for the warmer valleys lower on the mountain. Blue grouse spend the spring

At the base of Wheeler Peak, groves of aspen trees grow.

Limber pines and spruce trees grow on the higher slopes of Wheeler Peak.

and summer on the lower slopes. They come up the mountain for the winter. The buds and needles of Douglas fir trees will be winter food for them.

Higher up the slope, limber pines and Englemann spruce trees grow. The air is colder here, and the trees become smaller again. In the strong, bitter winds of the high country, trees grow low and twisted.

Porcupines find food in the high forest. They gnaw away the bark of trees to get at the inner bark underneath. Their quills keep them safe from most enemies. Birds live here, too. Red crossbills eat seeds of the fir, spruce, and pine trees.

FUN FACT Mule deer have a strange way of jumping called stotting. A mule deer moves along in a series of stiff-legged jumps, all four feet off the ground at the same time. When it lands, all four feet hit the ground together.

WHERE THE TREES END

High on the mountains trees cannot grow. But grass, moss, low bushes, and hardy plants can. Tiny six-inch *alpine* willow and flowers grow among the rocks. In the harsh winter cold and snow these low-lying plants survive.

Summer is short on the mountaintop. Snow covers the ground except for a few weeks. Then alpine meadows burst into bloom with plants like phlox, yellow buttercups, and Jeffrey shooting stars. The trail to Wheeler Peak leads past a sunny alpine meadow.

Mule deer and coyotes may visit the alpine tundra. Birds like Clark's nutcrackers and water pipits find food there. Mountain lions, bobcats, and rock squirrels prefer the high, rocky ground. Since winters are fierce and long, few animals can live on the mountaintop all year.

Bighorn sheep once ranged over the mountain peaks. But hunters shot the sheep, and cattle ate their food. The bighorn sheep disappeared.

Now bighorn sheep have been brought back into the park. High on the rocky slopes they climb, sure-footed and safe from enemies. During mating season, rams charge each other with their thick, curved horns. Horn to horn, two rams will crash together until ones gives up and goes away.

WHAT IS THE GREAT BASIN?

Great Basin National Park is part of the Snake Mountain Range. This range and more than 100 other mountain ranges sit in an area called the Great Basin. The ranges all lie in a north-south direction. Between them are long, flat stretches of sagebrush and desert.

These mountains lie between the Sierra Nevada Mountains of California on the west and the Wasatch Mountains of Utah on the east. This is the Great Basin. It covers almost all of Nevada, about half of Utah, and small parts of surrounding states.

What is different about the Great Basin? None of the rivers reach the sea. They all stay within the basin. Rivers that flow freely in the mountains dry up in the desert or collect in lakes like the Great Salt Lake. There is only one way water escapes the Great Basin. It evaporates. This area is one of the world's largest *internal drainage systems.*

FUN FACT Each basin in the Great Basin is filled with 6,000 to 10,000 feet of sand and clay from the mountains.

During the short summer season, alpine meadows bloom with color.

The Great Basin is part of a larger area called the *basin and range.* The basin and range reaches all the way down to Mexico. It includes Death Valley and the Mohave Desert.

Here the word "basin" means something different. It means the low valleys between mountains. Desert valleys separate the mountain ranges all through the area.

Some mountains are old and not growing. But the mountains in the Great Basin are young and still growing. They are only 17 million years old.

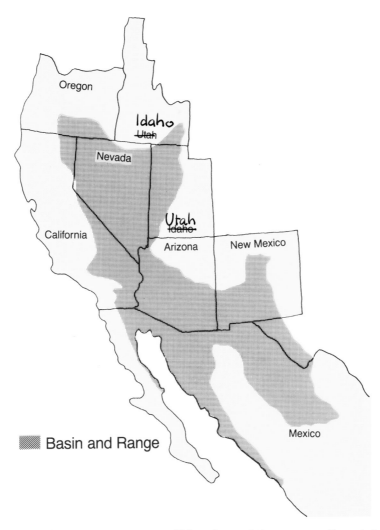

The basin and range covers most of Nevada and the surrounding states.

Bristlecones must endure harsh winters on Wheeler Peak.

HOW MOUNTAINS GROW

All oceans and continents ride on huge chunks of the earth's crust called *tectonic plates*. These plates move about. When they crash together they squeeze huge masses of rock into the sky. This is one way mountains are formed.

But in the Great Basin, something different is happening. The earth's crust is thin in this area because it is being lifted up and stretched apart. Because of this, the crust of the earth in the Great Basin has broken into blocks. The blocks have tipped, forcing one edge of the block high into the sky. The high edge forms the mountain range. The other edge of the block dives deep into the earth and forms the valley. The place where the blocks crack apart is called a *fault line*.

Great pressures pushing up underneath the earth cause earthquakes and hot springs. These are all signs of mountain building.

Hikers make their way through Great Basin's "cirque."

Other forces are tearing down the mountains. Rain, rivers, and ice wear them away. Like a huge basin, the valley collects the rock and sand that water washes down into it. As the basin fills and gets heavy, the blocks shift along the fault line. The mountain rises higher in the air, and the basin sinks.

Some *geologists* believe that one day this area will stretch open enough to let the Pacific Ocean in. The Great Basin will fill with water. California will become an island. This is not something to worry about. Changes such as these happen over millions of years.

GLACIERS—ICE AT WORK

During the Ice Age, huge sheets of ice called *glaciers* covered the northern part of North America. These great ice sheets never reached the Great Basin. But the area was much colder than it is today. Small mountain glaciers formed in the higher mountains of the Great Basin.

On the Snake Range, snow piled on top of snow. The layers became so deep that the buried snow turned into ice and started to move slowly down the mountainsides. These moving masses of ice and snow were glaciers. Glaciers picked up rocks and carried them along. They scraped away the earth and left huge piles of rubble called *moraines.*

In the park on Wheeler Peak there is a *cirque.* This is a bowl-shaped hollow carved out of a mountainside by a glacier. Moving ice broke off more and more rock and carried it away, leaving sheer rock walls nearly 2,000 feet high.

A small *ice field* lies at the bottom of the cirque near a bristlecone pine grove. An ice field may look like a glacier, but it does not move. This ice field may be the beginning of a new glacier. Geologists are not sure.

Six lakes nestle in the mountains of the park. Thousands of years ago, glaciers dug out the lake beds. Now melting snow and springs feed the lakes. Stella Lake is so shallow it freezes solid in the winter. Bighorn sheep sometimes graze on the rocky cliffs around Johnson Lake.

THE FIRST PEOPLE

During the Ice Age, much of the earth's water was locked up in giant mountains of ice. The seas were lower. People could walk across the land

Stella Lake is only one of the many lakes nestled in the mountains of Great Basin.

During the summer months, the base of Wheeler Peak is covered with greenery.

that joined Asia to North America. This is how people first came to North America.

Scientists have found animal bones, arrow points, and other stone tools in the Great Basin. These objects show that people must have lived or hunted there at least 11,000 years ago.

The land looked very different then. Instead of desert, the land was covered with grass and lakes. But the climate changed. Slowly the lakes dried up. People found a different way to live in the harsh, dry climate. They moved from place to place gathering nuts, seeds, berries, and roots. They hunted jackrabbits and other small animals.

These people lived in a delicate balance with the land. Seeds, nuts, and berries ripened first on the lower slopes. As the wave of summer moved up the mountains, other plants ripened. The people followed the harvest up the mountains. This way they could collect enought to eat. Piñon nuts were an important food.

The people stayed either in caves or in shelters they made out of sagebrush. They lived in small groups. Sometimes they gathered together for an antelope hunt, the piñon nut harvest, or a rabbit drive.

Because they moved around so much, the people had few belongings. They had milling stones to grind their seeds and roots into flour. They wove baskets and used them to gather seeds and nuts. They lined some baskets with pitch from piñon pine trees. The pitch made the baskets watertight. Then they could be used to carry water or for cooking.

For thousands of years these people lived on the land, and it nourished them.

ANOTHER KIND OF PEOPLE

About 1,000 years ago, another kind of people lived near what is now Great Basin National Park. They grew corn, squash, and beans near rivers and mountain valleys where there was enough water. They gathered wild plants and hunted deer and sheep in the mountains.

The remains of one of their villages were found near Baker, Nevada, outside the park. These people lived in homes that were dug in the ground like basements. Their homes were lined with sun-dried bricks, called *adobe*, and roofed. They stored their food in *granaries*. During the harsh winters they may have lived in caves of the Snake Range. Chipped stone tools, mammal bones, bits of flint, crude pottery, and fire-cracked rocks tell of their lives.

Inside the caves they left *pictographs*—pictures painted on rock in red, brown, and black. There are paintings of Rocky Mountain sheep, stick figures of people, and simple shapes like circles, dots, and lines. There are also pictures of human hands painted in red.

Some of their pictographs can still be seen in a cave not far from Lehman Caves. These caves are now under the care of the park. Visitors must be careful not to harm these ancient pictures. No one could ever repair such damage.

These people lived in the Snake Valley for at least 700 years. They grew their crops, hunted game, and gathered roots, seeds, and berries. Then suddenly they disappeared. Perhaps a long time without rain made farming impossible. They may have left when new tribes moved into the area, and there wasn't enough food for everyone. No one knows for sure why they left or where they went.

Six hundred years ago present-day Native American tribes were in the Great Basin. Snake, Goshute, Shoshone, and Paiute tribes lived in the valleys that are part of the park today. They gathered food and hunted animals in the mountains. When white people moved west into the Great Basin, the Native American way of life changed forever.

EXPLORERS OF THE GREAT BASIN

In 1827, Jedediah Strong Smith crossed the Great Basin near the Snake Range. He was a fur trapper looking for new areas to trap beaver. He also was searching for a great river. Some people thought this river flowed through the Great Basin to the Pacific Ocean. He never found such a river, nor did he find the beaver fields he had hoped for.

Between 1843 and 1845, John Fremont was sent by the government to map this land. He crossed the desert and mountains. He saw mountain peaks covered with snow and valleys covered with grass. He found plenty of deer and mountain sheep to feed his men. He was the first white person to describe the piñon pine.

John Fremont realized that none of the rivers in this area flowed to the sea. They stayed within, like water held in a bowl or basin. So he named the area the Great Basin.

After the Mexican War in 1848, the United States bought the Great Basin and other land from Mexico. It wasn't long before people flocked by the thousands over the vast American continent. Why? Because gold had been found in California.

To help the weary travelers get across the desert, relief trains, bringing fresh supplies, were sent from California. Soon trading posts were set up. People came to settle, to farm, and to raise cattle in the desert.

When William Prouse found gold in Nevada in 1850, people rushed back

FUN FACT In 1871 in White Pine County, a cup of coffee and a steak cost $1. A hay mattress bed, with blankets and some crickets thrown in, was $1. Apples were 25 cents a piece and chickens were $5 apiece.

from California to dig for gold and get rich. Ranchers came to raise cattle and feed the new mining towns. They grazed their cattle on the land where Native American people once found seeds and roots. Miners cut down piñon trees and burned the wood.

Settlers spread out over Nevada. Absalom Lehman came to the Snake Valley in the late 1860s. Many different stories tell how one day he found a dark hole in the ground. This hole was the natural entrance of a cavern. Absalom Lehman had discovered a cave.

The sheer rock walls of Great Basin's cirque tower 2,000 feet high.

LEHMAN CAVES

Using a sledgehammer, Absalom Lehman opened up paths through his cave. By late 1885, ladders were in place. Lehman led visitors on candlelight tours that lasted up to eight hours. Along the way, some of the people left their names on the cave walls. In large chambers the size of ballrooms early visitors held square dances and weddings.

Lehman was not the first person to visit the cave. Ancient bones of at least a dozen humans were found in the cave near the entrance. No one knows who buried these bones.

Each room of the cave is different. Some rock formations remind people of elephant trunks and angel wings. Some have names like Old George and His Pet Dog Spot. One formation looks like a parachute. People have looked at the rocks and seen a python, a poodle, and a sailor kissing his girlfriend. Visitors can still see this cave today.

HOW A CAVE IS FORMED

How did this beautiful cave come to be? Five hundred million years ago this area was covered by a great sea. Sand, mud, and the shells from tiny sea creatures built up layer upon layer. These layers hardened into rock.

About 17 million years ago the crust of the earth cracked into blocks. The blocks tipped, pushing up the mountain ranges.

Between one and five million years ago the cave began to form. Water that contained carbon dioxide filled the cracks in the rock. The carbon dioxide made the water acid. This water slowly dissolved the softer rock. Small cracks became huge caverns with tunnels between them.

Then the climate changed. The cave was left dry and ready for the next step. This step is still going on. Water drips into the cave and oozes through cracks in the walls. In the still air of the cave, the carbon dioxide bubbles out of the water. Crystals form. These crystals grow into different shapes called *dripstone*. Drip by drip, the water forms icicle shapes called *stalactites* on the ceiling of the cave. Where the drips of water fall to the floor of the cave, *stalagmites* rise. Over thousands of years, stalactites and stalagmites have grown and changed into beautiful formations.

FUN FACT   One tall tale about the discovery of Lehman Caves tells how Absalon Lehman was driving cattle in the Snake Range when his horse fell into a hole. In the story, Lehman held the horse between his knees for three days to keep it from falling into the cave.

In 1922, the cave was made a national monument to protect its fragile beauty.

LIFE UNDERGROUND

Many animals make their homes in the darkness of caves. Some, like pack rats, bats, and mice, are guests in the cave. They sleep there during the day or night, but they must leave to find food. If these animals were trapped

Rangers guide visitors through the beautiful underground world of Lehman Caves.

Lexington Arch may have been part of an old cave that is now worn away.

inside the cave, they could not survive.

Some animals, like beetles and crickets, could live outside caves. But they spend their whole lives underground. The food they eat is carried in by water, air, or other animals.

Some animals are only found in caves. They could not survive up in the sunshine. One unusual animal in Lehman Caves is the pseudoscorpion (pronounced sōō-dō-skor-pē-an). Less than an inch long, this animal is more like a spider than a scorpion. With its slender arms it sways through the cave searching for smaller animals or *fungi* to eat.

Animals that live underground have changed to live in darkness. Some have no color. Many are blind. Sight is useless in the blackness of a cave, so other senses have taken over. Hearing, smell, and touch help animals find their way around. Pack rats use long whiskers to feel their way.

Bats have trouble flying through the natural entrance of Lehman Caves because the entrance is a hole running straight down into the earth. But

To explore Little Muddy Cave, visitors must crawl through tight spaces and wear protective helmets.

spiders, fleas, flies, worms, pack rats, mice, and chipmunks all make their homes down in the dark.

LITTLE MUDDY CAVE

There are 30 or so other caves in the Snake Range. One of the caves in the park is Little Muddy. To visit Little Muddy Cave, a person must go with a ranger, be at least 14 years old, and like to crawl.

The door of the cave is only 11 inches high. People have to crawl on their bellies through many of its tunnels. The cold floors and walls are close and damp. There are only a few small stalactites hanging from the ceiling.

People must wear helmets to protect their heads. The headlamps on their helmets provide the only light in the intense darkness.

THE NAMING OF WHEELER PEAK

Wheeler Peak is the highest peak in the Snake Range. Over the years it has had several names.

Native Americans called it "Bia" and "Peup," meaning big.

A Mormon group called the White Mountain Mission explored the area in 1855. They sent several of their members to climb the highest peak. One of them was Ezra Granger Williams. He named it "Williams Peak," after himself.

"I tell you we were high up in the world," Williams wrote. "The air was so light and buoyant. We felt first rate.... We could see mountain after mountain to the west."

Three years later, Mormons sent out a second mission. They left a farming party in the Snake Valley. But the farmers did not stay long.

In 1859, J.H. Simpson, an Army explorer, renamed it "Union Peak." During the Civil War, local people dubbed it "Jeff Davis." Jefferson Davis was the president of the southern states.

When the war was over, the Army sent out another group led by Lt. J.M. Wheeler. Wheeler and some of his men climbed the mountain. A.F. White,

FUN FACT The bones of rabbits, squirrels, birds, and over 100 porcupines have been found in the Lost River passage of Lehman Caves. At one time this passage must have been open to the outside.

The view from the top of Wheeler Peak is spectacular!

a geologist, was in the party. He named the peak for Wheeler. That is the name it bears today.

A SIX-STORY ARCH AND A GOLD MINING DITCH

In the 1950s, local people heard rumors of a large stone arch. It was "big enough to ride a horse under." They went looking and found a limestone arch six stories high. The arch reaches 120 feet from end to end.

Lexington Arch is down a one-mile trail at the south end of the park. The arch may be a part of an old cave that has worn away. Now the arch is exposed above ground.

Osceola Ditch runs through the park. It was part of the mining boom in the late 1800s. When the boom was over, many ghost towns were left behind. One of them, Osceola, is in the northern end of the Snake Range, outside the park. In the early days of white settlement, this was a busy mining town. A 25-pound gold nugget was once found in Dry Gulch, near Osceola. Today there is still a little mining in this area.

PICTURES ON ROCKS

In the Snake Mountains there are pictures that have been chipped or scratched onto stone slabs that are scattered on the ground. They are different from the pictographs, which are painted on rock. These chipped and scratched pictures are called *petroglyphs*.

Some petroglyphs are 3,000 years old. There are many different styles and designs.

The Native Americans living in the area today do not know who made the petroglyphs. Hunters may have made them to mark game trails or to lure animals to the area. No one can be sure.

There are designs that look like mountain sheep, humans, a ten-legged lizard, a sun disc, bird tracks, and snakes. There are also circles, lines, spirals, rectangles, and dots. The petroglyphs and any other traces of ancient people are under the care of the park. They are protected by law.

THE MAKING OF A PARK

Great Basin National Park has been a long time in the making. In the 1920s a bill was written to make Wheeler Peak a national park. Over the years there were three more attempts to make this area a park.

But there were mining claims on the land. Ranchers grazed their cattle there. Many people fought against a park.

In 1979 a large mining company moved away. Many people lost their jobs. A new park could mean more tourists and more jobs. An agreement was reached. Mining claims could still be worked inside a park. Ranchers could still graze cattle on park land. In fact, the new park would be the only national park where cattle could always graze.

On October 27, 1986, President Reagan signed a bill making Great Basin the 49th national park. It is the first national park in Nevada. Now the ancient bristlecone pines and a part of the basin and range country are preserved forever.

THINGS TO DO

There are many things to see and do at Great Basin National Park. Be sure to stop by the visitor's center for more information. Here are a few ideas:

Tour Lehman Caves.

Take a nature walk with a ranger.

Hike the Bristlecone Icefield trail. See bristlecone pines thousands of years old. The trail also leads to the Wheeler cirque and the ice field.

If you are in good condition, you can hike the Wheeler Summit trail to the highest peak in the park. From the top you can see into Utah. If the sky is clear, you can see the Wasatch Mountains 150 miles away.

Fish in one of the mountain streams.

Visit the historic Rhodes Cabin. See exhibits about the caves. Follow the short trail that begins near the cabin and see the piñon forest.

Drive and hike to Lexington Arch.

Ski in winter.

Picnic and camp in four different campgrounds.

Drive along Wheeler Peak Scenic Drive in the summer (snow can close the road from October to July).

FUN FACT Early visitors to Lehman Caves were given a candle and promise that someone would come looking for them if they did not come out.

Visitors can enjoy the beauty of Great Basin National Park all year round.

Hike along Baker Creek to Baker Lake, tucked into a cirque the glaciers carved. If you go in the autumn, you will see a spectacle of colored leaves.

Follow the Alpine Loop trail to see two lakes formed by glaciers—Stella Lake and Teresa Lake.

Enjoy the quiet of this great wilderness.

TAKING CARE

Visitors need to care for the park and follow the rules. Here are some things to remember to help protect yourself and the park:

Stay on the trails. Careless footsteps can crush plants that took years to grow.

Don't bring a pet. If you do, it must be on a leash at all times. It may not go on the trails, into the backcountry, to the visitor's center, or on any activities led by a ranger.

Don't pick flowers.

Leave animals alone. They are wild animals. Do not feed or bother them.

Buy a Nevada fishing license before you go fishing.

Do not drink water from the mountain streams unless it has been boiled for five minutes. Mountain water can carry disease. Drinking water can be found in some camps and at the visitor's center.

Use only dead twigs and branches from fallen trees for campfires. Dead standing trees are important homes for wildlife. Do *not* collect dead bristlecone wood. This wood is a valuable record of history.

Bring water for hiking. Take at least a quart of water for each person even on short walks.

Backpackers should bury human waste at least 100 feet from any water source.

Wear sturdy boots or shoes for hiking. Many trails have sharp rocks.

Carry warm clothes and rain gear in the mountains. Be prepared for sudden storms.

Wear warm clothes to explore caves. Stay on the trail while in the cave. Do not touch the walls or any formation.

A permit is required to enter any cave in the park except Lehman Caves.

Be aware of avalanches on the mountain trails in winter and spring. Skiers should check for weather conditions and register before going out.

Snowstorms are possible in the mountains all year around.

Hypothermia is a danger if the weather turns wet or cold. A person's entire body temperature is lowered. People can become confused and drowsy, and can even die.

Many trails are strenuous. The air is thinner high in the mountain. Hikers may huff and puff. Walk slowly and take it easy. Mountain sickness comes about by going too high too fast. The warning signs are: trouble breathing, upset stomach, headache, extreme tiredness, and drowsiness. This is a serious condition. The only cure is to come down to a lower level.

National parks are set aside to protect the land. We are a part of the land. We need to work to save the land for ourselves and all living things of the earth.

PIÑON-NUT COOKIE RECIPE

People still eat piñon nuts (also called pine nuts). Here is a recipe for pine-nut cookies:

1 cup butter
¼ cup confectioner's sugar
2 cups flour
1 tsp. nutmeg
2 tsp. vanilla
1 tsp. cinnamon
1 Tablespoon water
1 cup chopped piñon nuts (pine nuts). Pecans, almonds, or walnuts can be used instead.

Cream butter and sugar. Add the flour, 1 tablespoon water, vanilla, cinnamon, nutmeg, and nuts and mix well. Shape into small balls and place on cookie sheets. Bake at 325° for 15 to 20 minutes. Coat with confectioner's sugar while still warm. Makes five to six dozen.

FOR MORE PARK INFORMATION

For more information about Great Basin National Park, write to:

White Pine County Chamber of Commerce
Box 239
Ely, NV 89301

Superintendent
Great Basin National Park
Baker, NV 89311

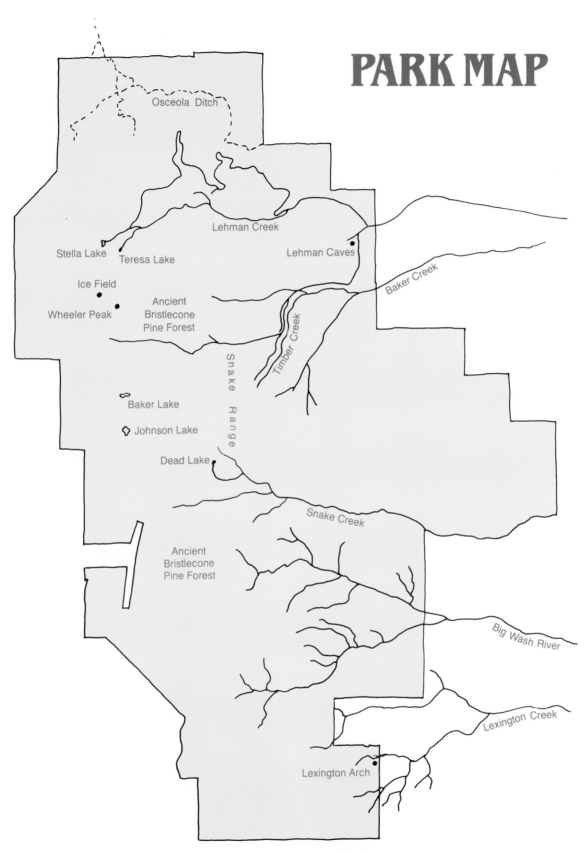

PARK MAP

Osceola Ditch

Lehman Creek

Stella Lake
Teresa Lake
Lehman Caves

Ice Field
Baker Creek

Ancient
Bristlecone
Pine Forest

Wheeler Peak

Snake Range

Timber Creek

Baker Lake

Johnson Lake

Dead Lake

Snake Creek

Ancient
Bristlecone
Pine Forest

Big Wash River

Lexington Creek

Lexington Arch

Great Basin National Park

GLOSSARY/INDEX

ADOBE *29* —Clay bricks dried by the sun and used by desert people to build homes and granaries.

ALPINE *13, 20, 43* —Referring to high mountains.

BASIN AND RANGE *5, 23* —A large region of the western United States made up of many mountain ranges divided by desert valleys.

BRISTLECONE PINE *5, 6, 25, 41, 43* —A type of pine tree. These trees are the oldest known living things on earth.

CIRQUE *25, 41, 43* —A bowl-shaped hollow scooped out of a mountain by a glacier.

CLIMATE *13, 28, 32* —The general or average weather in an area.

DRIPSTONE *32* —Crystals of calcium carbonate deposited by dripping water in the form of stalactites or stalagmites.

FAULT *24, 25* —A crack in the crust of the earth along which rock shifts up or down or side to side.

FUNGUS (PL. FUNGI) *36* —A kind of plant that cannot make its own food and must live off other plants. Molds, mildews, mushrooms and yeast are fungi.

GEOLOGIST *25, 40* —A person who studies the history of the earth and its changes as recorded in rocks and rock formations.

GLACIER *5, 25, 43* —A huge mass of ice that moves slowly over the land.

GRANARIES *29* —Storehouses for grain.

HYPOTHERMIA *44* —A dangerous body condition caused by becoming too cold. Over-all body temperature drops; severe hypothermia can cause death.

ICE FIELD *25, 41* —A mass of ice and snow that does not move.

INTERNAL DRAINAGE SYSTEM *20* —A land area where none of the water flows to the sea.

MORAINE *25* —A pile of sand, clay, or rocks left behind by a glacier.

PEAK *5, 30, 37* —The pointed top of a mountain. A mountain range can have many peaks separated by valleys, or several peaks can be bunched together.

PETROGLYPHS *40* —Pictures scratched, pecked, or cut into rocks by prehistoric people.

PICTOGRAPHS *29, 40* —Pictures painted on rocks by prehistoric people.

PYGMY FOREST *14, 15*—A forest of piñon pines and juniper trees that seldom grow more than 30 feet tall.

SAPLINGS *8*—Young trees.

STALACTITES *32, 37*—Icicles of stone that form on the ceiling of a cave. Dripping water forms stalactites and stalagmites.

STALAGMITES *32*—Pillars of stone that grow upward from the floor of a cave. Dripping water forms stalagmites and stalactites.

TECTONIC PLATES *24*—Huge slabs of the earth's crust that slowly drift about. Tectonics is the branch of geology that studies the movement of and changes in the earth's crust.

TREE LINE *6*—The imaginary line on a mountain beyond which trees cannot grow.